Creating an Emotionally Healthy Classroom

Practical and creative literacy and art resources for Key Stage 2

Daphne Gutteridge
and **Vivien Smith**

LONDON AND NEW YORK

First published 2010
by Routledge
2 Park Square, Milton Park, Abingdon, Oxon OX14 4RN

Simultaneously published in the USA and Canada
by Routledge
270 Madison Avenue, New York, NY 10016

Routledge is an imprint of the Taylor & Francis Group, an informa business

Typeset in Optima by Prepress Projects Ltd, Perth, UK
Printed and bound in Great Britain by CPI Antony Rowe,
Chippenham, Wiltshire

British Library Cataloguing in Publication Data
A catalogue record for this book is available from the British Library

Library of Congress Cataloging in Publication Data

Gutteridge, Daphne, 1948–
Creating an emotionally healthy classroom : practical and
creative PSHE, poetry, and literacy resource for key stage 2 /
Daphne Gutteridge and Vivien Smith.
p. cm.
Includes index.
1. Affective education—Great Britain. 2. Classroom
environment—Great Britain. 3. Poetry—Study and teaching
(Elementary)—Great Britain. 4. Art—Study and teaching
(Elementary)—Great Britain. I. Smith, Viv, 1951– II. Title.
LB1072.G88 2010
370.15'34—dc22
2009022498

ISBN 10: 0-415-49729-9 (hbk)
ISBN 10: 0-415-49728-0 (pbk)
ISBN 10: 0-203-86438-7 (ebk)

ISBN 13: 978-0-415-49729-9 (hbk)
ISBN 13: 978-0-415-49728-2 (pbk)
ISBN 13: 978-0-203-86438-8 (ebk)

We would like to dedicate this book to our families who have always provided unfailing support, our former colleagues and our lively and inspirational former pupils.

Contents

Figures

Acknowledgements

We would like to express our thanks to the following organisations for permission to reproduce the artworks in the book:

Awesome Art for supplying the following images and granting permission to reproduce them:

- *La Toilette* by Mary Cassatt
- *A Beautiful Flower* by Alma Taldema
- *Jockey flexed Forward Standing in the Saddle* by Edgar Degas
- *Carrier Pigeon* by Puvis de Chavannes
- *The Circus* by Georges Seurat
- *Four Poplars* by Claude Monet
- *Fighting Forms* by Franz Marc
- *Wheatfield with Rising Sun* by Vincent Van Gogh

Bridgeman Art Library for the following images:

- *The Great Day of Wrath* by John Martin

  Private Collection/ © Christopher Wood Gallery, London, UK/ The Bridgeman Art Library

- *The Boy* by Amedeo Modigliani

  Indianapolis Museum of Art, USA/ Gift of Mrs Julian Bobbs in memory of William Ray Adams/ The Bridgeman Art Library/out of copyright

- *Beata Beatrix* by Gabriel Rosetti

  Delaware Art Museum, Wilmington, USA/ Delaware Art Museum Acquisition Fund/ The Bridgeman Art Library/out of copyright

- *Arithmetic Composition* by Theo van Doesburg

  Felix Witzinger, Switzerland/ The Bridgeman Art Library/out of copyright

- *The Great Wave of Kanagawa* by Katsushika Hokusai

  Private Collection/ Lauros / Giraudon/ The Bridgeman Art Library/ out of copyright

The British Museum:

Thanks to the Trustees for the image of the Aztec Mask and copyright permission to reproduce it in the book.

Design and Artists Rights Copyright Society thanks to Cassandra King for granting copyright permissions for:

- *La Danse* by Henri Matisse

  Matisse: © Succession H Matisse/DACS 2009

- *Flight of the Swallows* by Giacomo Balla

  Balla: © DACS 2009

Nashford Publishing for the image of Henry VIII and copyright permission to use it in our book.

The National Trust for Scotland:

Thanks to Antonia Reece for the image of the *Hillhouse Chair* and copyright permission to use it in the book.

Many thanks to Sarah Kennedy and Sarah Woods and the pupils of St Cuthbert's RC Primary School, Pemberton in Wigan, whose artwork has been used to create the cover of the book.

Preface

As two very experienced primary school teachers we shared a class of primary pupils for over ten years. We have since worked extensively in the field of education and are very encouraged that the current vision for education in the United Kingdom is recognising the importance of the social and emotional aspects of learning. This has always been central to our own core beliefs for children's education and underpinned all our practice in schools.

The artwork which has been used to create the cover of the book was produced by the pupils of St Cuthbert's RC Primary School, Pemberton in Wigan. The pupils attended an art club run by two final year trainees from Edge Hill University, Sarah Kennedy and Sarah Woods. They used 'Emotions' as the stimulus for the work they produced. The pupils were obviously very engaged with the activity as the following comments show:

> I think it was easy and fun to show our emotions through art because we could use different colours, materials and patterns.
>
> (Keanu Y4)

> Happy is my favourite emotion to paint and create because I'm always smiling.
>
> (Rachel Y4)

> We had to imagine our feelings and emotions so we could create our artwork.
>
> (Kaya Y4)

> I liked painting outside, it was fun and made me laugh, I felt happy so it was easy to create a happy feeling picture.
>
> (Louise Y6)

We hope this book will help to inspire and motivate other teachers to make social and emotional wellbeing of pupils an integral part of their own teaching.

Introduction

This book is designed to help practitioners who are committed to creating an emotionally healthy environment in which pupils feel valued, have a sense of belonging and feel confident in expressing their thoughts and feelings.

There is very convincing evidence to suggest that if we develop emotional literacy in pupils this will lead to improved wellbeing, self-esteem, positive relationships and higher achievement. Therefore, schools are continually exploring ways to successfully place emotional literacy at the heart of teaching and learning.

What is emotional literacy?

Katherine Weare in her book *Developing the Emotionally Literate School* (2004) defines it as:

> The ability to understand ourselves and others and to be aware of, understand and to use information about the emotional states of others with competence. It includes the ability to understand, express and manage our own emotions, and respond to the emotions of others, in ways that are helpful to both ourselves and others.

Currently, schools are addressing these issues through PSHE (Personal Social and Health Education) supported by the SEAL (social and emotional aspects of learning) programme.

What is SEAL?

This is a programme which offers a whole school framework for promoting the social and emotional aspects of learning. These are defined as five broad areas of learning:

- Self-Awareness – pupils need to know how they learn, how they relate to others, what they are thinking and feeling.
- Managing Feelings – pupils need to be able to use, recognise and accept their feelings. They can use this to regulate their learning and behaviour.
- Motivation – pupils need to take an active and enthusiastic part in learning, know how to set themselves goals and work towards them, how to focus and concentrate on learning and how to persist in learning when this proves difficult.
- Empathy – pupils need to know how to understand others, anticipate and predict their likely thoughts, feelings and perceptions. They learn to see things from another point of view and modify their response accordingly.
- Social Skills – pupils need to know how to relate to others, take an active part in a group, communicate with different audiences, negotiate and resolve differences.

When pupils have good social and emotional skills and are in a supportive emotional environment, they will be more able to:

- deal with conflict;
- manage strong feelings;
- be calm and optimistic;
- recover from setbacks;
- keep going when things are difficult;
- understand and respect differences.

However, if children feel:

- awkward;
- anxious;
- embarrassed;
- stressed;
- angry;
- frustrated;
- excluded

it will then be more difficult for them to:

- pay attention;
- concentrate on a task;
- be creative;
- work within a group;
- be motivated and interested;
- keep going when things get difficult.

Emotional health and wellbeing creates happier, healthier children who do better in learning and in life and is an important strand of the Personal Social and Health Education (PSHE) curriculum in schools.

What is Personal Social and Health Education?

Personal Social and Health Education includes everything schools do to promote pupils' good health and wellbeing to develop mature, independent and self-confident pupils with an awareness and respect for others. It is also backed by the National Healthy Schools programme and links very strongly with the Every Child Matters Agenda.

How do we encourage children to explore their emotions?

It is often difficult to verbalise our feelings or emotions and express them with confidence. This book has been written to offer alternative opportunities to encourage discussion and self-awareness of personal emotions as well as developing empathy with others and how and why pupils may be feeling as they do. Through our own extensive teaching experience, we know that interactive activities are far more likely to engage and stimulate pupils, therefore enriching their thinking and learning.

Personal Social and Health Education can be delivered as a discrete lesson but it permeates all practice in schools. Aspects of pupils' social and emotional development are developed across the whole school curriculum and the work presented in this book will support teachers in this area of their practice.

Why a cross-curricular approach?

Current educational thinking supports cross-curricular teaching as a way of increasing children's motivation for learning and their level of engagement. Children are able to see the value of what they are learning so become more actively involved. This book provides ample opportunities for the practitioner to take a creative approach in supporting children's exploration of their emotions, not only through PSHE but also through poetry and art. Through a range of fun activities in all these curriculum areas we hope to stimulate creativity.

What is creativity?

Creativity has been interpreted in many ways, but the National Curriculum outlines the importance of creativity as follows:

> By providing rich and varied contexts for pupils to acquire, develop and apply a broad range of knowledge and understanding and skills, the curriculum should encourage pupils to think creatively and critically . . . Creative pupils lead richer lives and, in the longer term, make a valuable contribution to society.

In September 2000, the National Advisory Committee on Creative and Cultural Education produced a report entitled *All our Futures*. The report recognised the importance of creativity as multi-dimensional, which involves using imagination, being original and judging value. The report states:

> Creative and cultural education provide ways of engaging with issues of social change. They enable schools to address such consequences of change and alienation and exclusion, and to raise young people's self-esteem and motivation.

We would maintain that the opportunities for interaction and discussion with children, as laid out in this text, offer support to teachers who care deeply about their pupils and their development.

Layout and approach

This aspect of emotional literacy may be delivered in other areas of the curriculum or as a specific PSHE lesson. However, this book offers the practitioner a resource which could be used in several different ways:

- as a stimulus for PSHE discussion;
- as part of a literacy lesson;
- as part of an art lesson;
- as a cross-curricular literacy/art/PSHE lesson;
- as a resource book for a series of lessons on the topic of emotions;
- as a resource to support the SEAL programme;
- as stimulus for a Circle Time discussion;
- as an artist information text;
- as a poetry book.

Included in each session are the relevant learning objectives and also specific curriculum links to PSHE, SEAL, Renewed Literacy Framework, and Programmes of Study for Art and Design, as well as to any other appropriate cross-curricular opportunities.

Although the art images are reproduced in black and white, web links are given to enable teachers to display the original artworks on the interactive whiteboard.

Art and design

Pieces of artwork have been carefully chosen, which can in some way illustrate each emotion. The works range from pre-Raphaelite to modern art installations and represent a wide variety of artists and craftspeople. Clear headings mean that teachers can see at a glance which area of art the linked activities cover and also the resources needed. A list of artists and artworks has been added so teachers are able to use the activities when studying the work of a particular artist.

Art and design offers a perfect opportunity for children to explore their feelings in a creative, personal and non-threatening way. Looking at the works of a variety of artists, craftspeople and designers from a range of times and cultures encourages children to communicate their ideas and feelings. It helps to develop their critical awareness and respect for others' work and can sometimes challenge their own attitudes and values in relation to images. The practical art activities give opportunities for children to experiment with a variety of methods and approaches, tools and techniques and provide stimulating starting points to help develop creativity and imagination in their work and their thinking.

Literacy

The poems have been especially written to convey each of the emotions covered in the book, so are ideal to give opportunities for thought and discussion. Following each poem are linked literacy activities, ranging from drama to performance to written pieces incorporating work from the New Literacy Framework.

The New Literacy Framework places greater emphasis on speaking and listening. Most teachers would agree that for children to be able to speak and express themselves clearly and develop active listening strategies equips them with extremely important life skills. The use of the 'think, pair, share' technique incorporated in the literacy activities helps children to develop these skills by giving them opportunities to express themselves in a way that does not involve sharing their thoughts and feelings with the rest of the class, if they choose not to do so. It also encourages them to explore their ideas in more depth and gives every child equal participation and simultaneous interaction.

Poetry is an effective device to use with children as through it they can learn how complex thoughts, humorous ideas and deep emotions are expressed with a few, carefully chosen words. Poetry can access areas of imagination, which can contribute to children growing as critical thinkers. The book contains a variety of poetic forms and genres that encourage children to rethink what a poem is whilst offering them short pieces of writing, which will help sustain their interest.

Positive emotions

Learning objectives

The following learning objectives relate to the renewed Primary Literacy Framework. Objectives from the framework that are specific to each session appear in the text box at the top of each unit, but all the sessions in this book will enable practitioners to address the following learning outcomes:

Speaking

To be able to:

1a) Offer reasons and evidence for their views considering alternative opinions.

1b) Respond to the contributions of others in the light of differing viewpoints.

1c) Use the technique of dialogic talk to explore ideas, topics or issues.

Listening and responding

To be able to:

2b) Follow up others' points and show they agree or disagree in whole class discussion.

Group discussion and interaction

To be able to:

3c) Use the language of possibility to investigate and reflect on feelings, behaviour or relationships.

All the sessions will also enable practitioners to address the following learning outcomes from the Programme of Study for Art and Design. Objectives from the framework that are specific to individual sessions appear in the text box at the top of each unit.

Investigating and making

To be able to:

2c) Use a variety of methods and approaches to communicate observational ideas and feelings and design and make images and artefacts.

Knowledge and understanding

To know about:

4a) Visual and tactile elements including colour, pattern and texture, line and tone shape, form and space.

4b) Materials and processes used in making art and design.

4c) Differences and similarities in the work of artists, craftspeople and designers in different times and cultures (for example sculptors, photographers, architects and textile designers).

1 Brave

Curriculum Links: PSHE 1b 1c **SEAL: Good to be Me**

Literacy: 1a 1b 1c 2b 3c

Learning objectives

- to develop empathy and build self-esteem;
- to be able to create a poem based on experience and using a given format.

Today I'm gonna be brave.
I'm gonna jump in the deep end of the pool
And not care how long it takes to come up.

Today I'm gonna be brave.
When Marvinder Basanti calls me names,
I'm gonna tell him to get lost!

Today I'm gonna be brave.
I'm gonna answer every question
Even though they might not be right.

Today I'm gonna be brave.
I'm gonna tell Sharon Peters
I think she's really cool.

Today I'm gonna be brave.
I'm gonna admit to my teacher
That I don't understand decimals.

Today I'm gonna be brave.
My lips aren't going to quiver
When I don't get in the footy team.

Today I'm gonna be brave.
And sit next to Billy Taylor
On the way home.

Today I'm gonna be brave.
Well . . .
I think I am!

Vivien Smith

- Ask the pupils if they can empathise with any of the scenarios in the poem. Discuss with their partner. Share their experiences with the class if appropriate.
- Ask them what the last line of the poem means. How was the poet feeling at this point?
- Ask the pupils if they think it is always easy to feel brave. Why/why not?
- Ask if anyone would like to share a time when they were particularly brave.

Further follow-up activities: poetry writing

Ask the pupils to think of their own scenarios and create their own poem using the same format as the one they have just read. They can end it any way they choose.

Art: 2c 4a 4b 4c

Learning objectives

- to compare and contrast work by a variety of artists on the same theme;
- to develop design and collage skills through the construction of figures.

Christ on the Cross by Georges Henri Rouault

This painting is a large image of Christ on the Cross with 3 figures standing surrounding the Cross. It is a stylized image, with glowing colours and heavy black lines which are reminiscent of a stained glass window.

Georges Henri Rouault 1871–1958 was a French expressionist painter. He was born in Paris to a poor family and was apprenticed to a glass blower at the age of fourteen. His early experience there has been suggested as the likely source of his later paintings. The heavy black lines and glowing colours in his work are reminiscent of stained glass.

Web image: Use Wikipedia (www.wikipedia.org). Type 'Rouault' into the search box. On the Rouault page scroll down to online resources and click on 'Works by Georges Rouault'. The image appears as *Christ en Croix*.

- What is this image depicting? How is it linked to the theme of bravery?
- How do you think this image was produced? Where might you expect to see an image like this?
- Why do you think the artist has used such bright colours, even though the subject matter is quite sad?
- Why do you think the artist also added several black outlines?
- How is this different to the more traditional images of the crucifixion?
- Which do you prefer and why? (The teacher could perhaps show some traditional images.)

Further follow-up activities: drawing, design and collage

Resources: selection of crosses, a wooden manikin if available, pencils, coloured pencils, coloured paper, scissors and glue

- Look at a selection of crosses (Celtic, St Andrew's, St George's, etc.) and discuss.
- Ask the pupils to design their own cross. Draw a large image onto A3 paper.
- Show pupils a manikin if possible and let them observe how the parts of the body are shaped. Ask them to cut out some body parts from coloured paper. Place onto A3 paper around the cross to create figures. (There is no need to add facial features.)

2 Calm

Curriculum Links: PSHE: 1a 1d SEAL: Good to be Me

Literacy: 1a 1b 1c 2b 3c

Learning objectives

- to understand and reflect upon the importance of positive emotions;
- to understand the meaning and use of alliteration and synonyms.

A mirror image of trees
Magically appears in the glassy water.
No ripples to break the spell
Or circling sounds of birds,
No chatter of children
Or a fisherman's delighted shout
Disturbs the perfect peace.
Tranquility and calm stills my restless body
And reflects in my eyes and my mind.
This silent moment in time
Is mine.

Vivien Smith

- Is it good to feel calm? Why?
- What other kinds of places or things make you feel calm?
- Ask the pupils if they can remember what alliteration means. Ask for examples from the poem.
- Why do they think the poet may have a 'restless body'?
- What has helped calm the poet?

Further ideas for follow-up work: using a thesaurus – synonyms

- Can the pupils think of any expressions using the word 'calm'? For example, calm before the storm; all is calm; calm my nerves; calming effect; etc.
- Give out cut-out head shapes. Ask the pupils in groups to fill the head with any words from the poem that relate to being calm. Include any other words or phrases you know. Use a thesaurus to find synonyms which can also be included. Share ideas.

Art: 4a 4b 4c

Learning objectives

- to recognise how artists create mood in their paintings;
- to learn about Impressionist paintings.

Claude Monet was a French painter who was devoted to painting outdoors. He was the initiator and leader of the Impressionist style of painting. The Impressionist style was characterised chiefly by concentrating on a general impression produced by the scene or object and using unmixed primary colours.

Web image: www.awesome-art.biz. Click on 'Monet and Manet'. Scroll down the page to list of titles and click on *Four Poplars*.

- What mood has Monet created in this painting?
- How has he managed to create this mood?
- What time of day do you think he portrayed in this painting?
- How does it make you feel?
- What do we mean by a 'mirror image'? What is another word for this term?

Further follow-up activities: painting

Resources: A3 paper, a selection of paints and brushes

- Think of something or somewhere that gives you a feeling of calm. Design a picture based on this.
- Use A3 size paper. Fold it in half horizontally. On the top part paint your picture based on your design. Carefully fold the paper in order to give a reflection of your picture on the lower half.

Figure 1 *Four Poplars* by Claude Monet. Reproduced with permission of Awesome Art.

Confident

Curriculum Links: PSHE 1b 1c **SEAL: Good to be Me**

Literacy: 1a 1b 1c 2b 3c

Learning objectives

- to build pupil self-esteem;
- to investigate rhyme and alliteration in poetry.

I feel good today.
My shoulders relaxed,
My spine straight and strong,
I walk with the air of a person
Who is never wrong.
My eyes are bright,
There's a smile on my lips,
It's a good hair day,
There's a swagger to my hips.

Today I feel is going to be good.
I feel it in every bone
As I stride ahead
Into the unknown.
There's a shining path,
It's beckoning me.

Today I'm going to be
The very best that I can be

Vivien Smith

- Why do you think the poet may be feeling so good about themselves?
- Which line do you think best portrays their good mood? Why?
- Where do you think the 'shining path' may be leading to?
- Is there a rhyming scheme to this poem? Is it exactly the same in each verse?
- Does the poet use any alliteration? If so give some examples.

Further follow-up activities: speaking and listening and annotation

With talk partners discuss:

- Do you have days when you really feel good about yourself?
- What kind of things make you feel like this?
- Can you describe how you feel inside at these times?
- What kind of things might you be doing which would make you 'the best that I can be'?

Draw and annotate yourself when you are feeling really good about everything, for example, neat shiny hair, smiling, bright eyes, favourite clothes, etc.

Art: 2c 4a 4b 4c

Learning objectives

- to learn how stained glass windows are created;
- to learn how to produce an image to create a stained glass window effect.

Henry VIII was an accomplished scholar and a fine athlete. He was born in 1509 and died in 1547. He was married six times and fathered three children – Mary I, Edward VI and Elizabeth I. He split from the Church of Rome and established the Church of England so he would obtain a divorce from his first wife. He was the true founder of the British Navy and a true patron of learning. His people loved, trusted and honoured him throughout his life.

Web image: www.nashfordpublishing.co.uk. Click on 'image reproduction'. Scroll down the page and click on 'portraits'. Click onto 'Kings and Queens of England' and scroll down to the images of Henry VIII.

Figure 2 *Stained Glass Window of Henry VIII*. Reproduced with permission of Nashford Publishing.

- This is a stained glass window. Can anyone explain what that is? (Explanation appears in the Glossary.)
- Where would you most likely see stained glass windows?
- Do you think the king looks confident in this portrait? Why/why not?
- What object has the artist added to make him look even more important and confident?
- How is Henry standing? How does this add to his look of confidence?
- What are the predominant colours the artist has used? Why do you think the artist has used these colours in particular?
- How many different patterns can you see in this portrait?

Further follow-up activities: stained glass windows

Resources: coloured cellophane, black masking tape, scissors

Design a picture in the style of a stained glass window. Base it on a pattern (keep it simple because if it is very intricate, it will be too difficult to make with cellophane) and select which colours are going to be used. Decide where you are going to divide the pattern with black lines to imitate the look of a stained glass window. Using an A4 or A5 sheet of paper as a template, sketch out the pattern and where the black lines will be. Cut the cellophane accordingly and then piece together with masking tape. This is quite fiddly, but if masking tape is put on the other side as well the finished pictures can be stuck onto the windows and should give the appearance of stained glass.

Determined

Curriculum Links: PSHE 1a 1b **SEAL: Going for Goals**

Literacy: 1a 1b 1c 2b 3c

Learning objectives

- to develop an understanding of how being determined can be a positive emotion;
- to extend vocabulary;
- to develop skill in performance poetry.

Dedicated
Enthusiastic
Tenacious
Enduring
Resolute
Motivated
Indomitable
Never
Ever
Doubting

Vivien Smith

- What kind of poem is this? (acrostic)
- What effect does writing a poem in this way have?
- Can any of the children give a definition for the word 'determined'?

In turn take each of the first seven words and ask the children if they know the meanings of them. In pairs then ask the children to look them up in a dictionary and then, as a class, feed back the definitions that can be written down by the teacher.

- Do they notice anything about all the definitions?
- Are there any similarities?
- Which word do the children think best describes 'determined'? Why?

Further follow-up activities: performance poetry

With talk partners ask the children to discuss any times when they have felt really determined about something:

- How did it make them feel?
- Why did they feel like this?
- Share with the rest of the class.

Divide the class up into seven groups and perform the poem with everyone saying the last three words together. Ask the children to add a short phrase or sentence after each of the first seven words that describe being determined in some way, e.g. Dedicated . . . to my football team, Enthusiastic . . . about maths. Perform the poem again choosing a child to use their phrase to complete each line.

Art: 2c 4a 4b 4c

Learning objectives

- to introduce pupils to the work of Balla;
- to learn the technique of printing.

Figure 3 *Flight of the Swallows* by Giacomo Balla. Reproduced with permission of DACS, Balla: © DACS 2009.

Giacomo Balla was an Italian painter born in 1871. He died in 1958. As a child he studied music but by the age of twenty had decided to study painting at local academies. Futurism was an Italian art movement that wanted nothing of the past but admired speed and technology. Futurists practised in all mediums. Balla adopted a futurist style creating pictorial depictions of light, movement and speed. He also began sculpting in 1914, and during the First World War his studio became a meeting place for young artists.

Web image: Log onto www.orange.co.uk (or use your own preferred search engine, e.g. Google). Click on the images tab above the search box. Type in *The Flight of the Swallows* by Balla.

Let the children look at this painting in silence for a couple of minutes, then ask them what they can see in the picture:

- Can they count the number of birds they can see?
- How has the artist positioned the birds? Why do you think they were positioned like this? What effect does it have?
- In what way does this picture link to the word 'determined'?
- Do they like this picture? Why/why not?

Further follow-up activities: printing

Resources: sheets of perspex or glass (about A4 size), paint rollers, assorted paints or printing inks, A4 paper

Ask the children to choose an object or shape. Draw and cut out several of the objects/shapes. Experiment with placing the shapes onto A4 paper, they can be overlapping or individually placed. Cover the glass/perspex with paint using the roller. Then carefully position the shapes/images onto the paint. Next, gently place a piece of A4 paper on top and with a clean roller or a hand, roll or press the paper firmly. Carefully peel the paper off and there should be a white, stencilled image of the shapes surrounded by colour.

Excited

Curriculum Links: PSHE 1a 1e **SEAL: Going for Goals**

Literacy: 1a 1b 1c 2b 3c

Learning objectives

- to help everyone understand that excitement is a positive emotion but that we need to contain it sensibly;
- to able to recognise and write in a journalistic style.

Three days to go.
I can feel the glow
Spreading through me,
Until it reaches my face
And a smile as wide as space
Appears from nowhere.

Two days to go.
And though
I try to hide that smile,
It won't budge.
But no-one can see
The warm waves inside of me
Or hear the sound of glee
Ringing in my ears.

One day to go.
Time's so slow

But I can't keep the laughter in,
Or the grin
Playing on my lips.
I'm in the mood for fun
And I run in meaningless circles.

Here at last!
But now time moves so fast.
I need to remember each bit of it.
What's been the best?
The feeling of complete happiness.

Vivien Smith[1]

- Why do you think the poet was excited? What was she waiting for?
- How do you feel when you are excited? Have you ever felt or done any of the things described in the poem when you have been excited?
- Where is the most exciting place you have ever been? What made it exciting?
- In what situations is showing excitement not always appropriate? Why?

Further follow-up suggestions: journalistic writing

In pairs, think of an exciting event coming up (real or imaginary) and create a short news article with a heading/subheading, or alternatively an advertising flyer.

Art : 2c 4a 4b 4c

Learning objectives

- to learn what is meant by pointillisme;
- to use this technique in their own work.

[1] Reproduced with permission of Routledge from *Using Circle Time for PSHE and Citizenship*, Daphne Gutteridge and Vivien Smith (Routledge 2008)

Figure 4 *The Circus* by George Seurat. Reproduced with permission of Awesome Art.

Georges Seurat was born in 1859 and died in 1891. He developed 'Pointillisme'. He applied colour as dots or tiny detached strokes of pure colour which, when viewed from a distance, fused together to create subtle changes in form and made his paintings shimmer with brilliance. The Circus was painted in 1891.

Web image: www.ibiblio.org/wm/paint. Click on artist index and go to Seurat. Scroll to the final image on the page, *The Circus*, and click to load. Click on image to enlarge.

- What is going on in this painting?
- What noises do you think you would hear if you were there? Describe the atmosphere.
- Do you like the picture? Why/why not?

Further follow-up activities: creating pointillist painting

Resources: A4 paper, felt pens and/or paint and cotton wool buds

Use felt tip pens (or paint and cotton wool buds). Choose a person who excites you (e.g. a sportsman, a musician) or an object that represents them (e.g. a football, a guitar, etc.) and recreate a pointillist picture.

Happy

Curriculum links: PSHE 1b **SEAL: Good to be Me**

Literacy: 1a 1b 1c 2b 3c

Learning objectives

- to recognise and appreciate the feeling of happiness;
- to revise apostrophes of possession and omission and the use of exclamation marks;
- to recognise and be able to write in the form of rhyming couplets.

SMILE . . . I'm by the sea
And there's no-one here but me.
SMILE . . . I've won the game
And the crowd's shouting MY name!
SMILE . . . Friday at last!
All those tests are in the past.
SMILE . . . I'm on holiday
With nothin' to do – just play.
SMILE . . . I've made a new friend
Don't want this day to end!
SMILE . . . Christmas is near
Stocking full of new gear.
SMILE . . . going to gran's
Where my music's never been banned.

SMILE . . . school play's about to start
And I've got the starring part!

SMILE . . . favourite programme's on
And all my homework's done.
SMILE . . . that joke was great!
Can't wait to tell a mate.
SMILE . . . chips for tea!
SMILE . . . it's great to be . . .
ME!

Vivien Smith

- Which is your favourite line in the poem? Why?
- What is the rhyming scheme of the poem?
- How are the apostrophes used?
- Is there a difference between the apostrophe in 'gran's' and 'they've'? What is it? (Revise apostrophes of possession/omission.)
- Why do you think some lines end in an exclamation mark and others don't? What is the effect of the exclamation marks?
- Make a list of all the words with apostrophes and what they should read in full.

Further ideas for follow-up work: creating a rhyming class poem

- Smile at the class. Count how many pupils smile back at you.
- Can they guess what you're counting?
- Discuss with the class what the effect of someone smiling at you has.

With talk partners discuss what makes you happy. Feed back to the class.

In pairs children can compose a line each beginning: *Happiness is . . .* Try to make them rhyme. Encourage adding phrases or sentences not just a couple of words. Read around the class to create a class 'Happiness' poem.

Art: 2c 4a 4b 4c

Learning objectives

- to learn about the work of Henri Matisse;
- to learn how artists are able to create a particular mood in their work;
- to develop skill in working in 3D.

Figure 5 *La Danse* by Henri Matisse. Reproduced with permission of DACS Matisse: © Succession H Matisse/DACS 2009.

Henri Matisse (1869–1954) was a French artist who was renowned for his use of colour. He was a draughtsman, printmaker and sculptor but is principally known for his paintings. His mother first bought him art supplies in 1889 when he was recovering from appendicitis and he became an artist much to the disappointment of his father. He is one of the best known artists of the twentieth century. Initially he was a 'fauvist'. They were a group of painters who expressed emotion with wild dissonant colours without regard to the natural colour of the subject.

Web image: Use Wikipedia (www.wikipedia.org). Type 'Matisse' into the search box. Scroll down the page to 'paintings' and click onto *The Dance* (second version) Alternatively, log onto a search engine (Orange, Google, etc.) and click onto the images tab above the search box and type in *La Danse* by Henri Matisse. Click on one of the images to enlarge.

- What kind of mood has Matisse created in this painting?
- Why might the characters be feeling like this?
- Why do you think he has painted the figures without clothes?
- Why do you think Matisse has chosen to use such a plain background with limited colour?

Further ideas for follow-up work: 3D figures

Resources: a wooden manikin if possible, chicken wire, pliers, blocks of wood, nails, assorted materials to decorate (ribbon, tissue, string, etc.)

- If possible use manikins and look at how the shape of the body changes when moving.
- Look at pictures of moving figures, e.g. sportsmen, dancers, gymnasts.
- Using wire/chicken wire, create a 3D figure bending the body and/ or limbs to give a feeling of movement. Pliers may be needed. The figures could be mounted on small blocks of wood using u-shaped nails or could be suspended from the ceiling when finished. Pieces of material/ribbon/tissue/string, etc. could be added to the figures to add to the feeling of movement.

Hopeful

Curriculum Links: PSHE 4a 4b **SEAL: Good to be Me**

Literacy: 1a 1b 1c 2b 3c

Learning objectives

- to help pupils understand that they can develop a strategy to deal with negatives thoughts;
- to be able to create a poster which communicates a particular image.

Hold that image!
And with it a memory
To be banked
In the database of your mind.
To be retrieved
When you want to forget
A time that was unkind.

Vivien Smith

- What or who do you think was unkind to the poet?
- Can you describe the image the poet uses to help shut out negative thoughts?
- Can you think of a time when you felt life was being unkind to you?
- Have you got a place or time that conjures up a wonderful image in your mind?
- Describe it to your talking partner or write it down.

Further follow-up activities: design a poster

In pairs design a holiday poster which describes the destination as a 'paradise'.

Art: 2c 4a 4b 4c

Learning objectives

- to develop an understanding of tonal effect;
- to learn the technique of papier mâché and develop 3D work.

Pierre Puvis de Chavannes (1824–1898) was the foremost French mural painter of the late nineteenth century, whose works decorate many public buildings in France. His paintings were done on large canvases then fixed to walls (marouflage). He was well respected by many painters including Toulouse Lautrec and Seurat. He used simplified forms and non-naturalistic colours. The pale colours he used gave his murals the appearance of frescoes.

Web image: www.awesome-art.biz. Click on 'symbolism art'. Click on 'View all images on CD'. Use search box at the top of the page to enter *Carrier Pigeon* by Puvis de Chavannes.

- Why might the artist have used such a limited colour palette in the painting?
- What effect does the use of light and dark tones create?
- What can you see in this picture apart from the woman?
- Do you think she is feeling happy?
- What in the picture suggests she may be feeling hopeful?
- What do you think the woman is thinking at this moment?
- Where do you think the pigeon is going to or coming from?

Further follow-up activities: papier mâché flight balloons

Resources: balloons, yoghurt pots, newspaper, plain paper, glue, paint and string

- Design and make a flight balloon.
- Cover a real balloon with papier mâché (explanation in the Glossary). When the papier mâché is dry, paint it. Whilst it is drying

Figure 6 *Carrier Pigeon* by Pierre Puvis de Chavannes. Reproduced with permission of Awesome Art.

cover a yoghurt pot or margarine tub with paper and paint. Attach the pot to the balloon with string or wool so it looks like a balloon basket. Write down your hopes and dreams and put them in the balloon basket.

- These would make a great display hanging from the classroom ceiling.

Loved

Curriculum Links: PSHE 1b 4c **SEAL: Good to be Me**

Learning objectives

- to understand the difference being loved makes to your life;
- to recognise what a sonnet is and to introduce some of Shakespeare's work;
- to be able to write in the form of a sonnet.

I feel your arms around me
And the warmth of your love
Spreads through my body, right to its core.
I feel your hand clasping mine tightly
As if you'll never let it go
Your strength becomes my strength
I feel your lips brush the top of my head
And I am blessed that you are in my life.
Your love gives me power
Over the things of which I am unsure
And the confidence to walk tall
When sometimes I feel small
I smile contentedly
I know I am loved

Vivien Smith

- How does the poet know that they are loved?
- Who do you think the person giving the love is? (mother, father, friend?)

- How do you think being loved makes the poet feel?
- When someone feels loved, what difference does it make to their life?

Further ideas for follow-up work: writing a sonnet

- Explain what a sonnet is (fourteen-line poem, no specific rhyming pattern).
- William Shakespeare is famous for writing sonnets (e.g. *Shall I compare thee to a Summer's Day*).
- Pupils could compose their own love sonnet.

Art: 2c 4a 4b 4c

Learning objectives

- to learn about the work of Mary Cassatt;
- to improve observational drawing skills.

Mary Cassatt was an American painter who was born in 1844 and died in 1926. She studied art in Philadelphia then travelled extensively in Europe where she met and worked with the Impressionists. She was interested in pictures of everyday life, particularly the domestic and intimate. This picture was painted in 1891.

Web image: www.ibiblio.org/wm/paint. Use artist index to log onto the Mary Cassatt page. Scroll down to *La Toilette* and click on the image to enlarge.

- In this painting, how is the mother demonstrating her love for the child? Talk about the actions and the body language.
- Hands are often used to show love and affection. What other ways can they show love?
- How is the child responding to this demonstration of love?
- What part of everyday life might an artist use today if they wanted to create the same intimate picture of a mother and child?

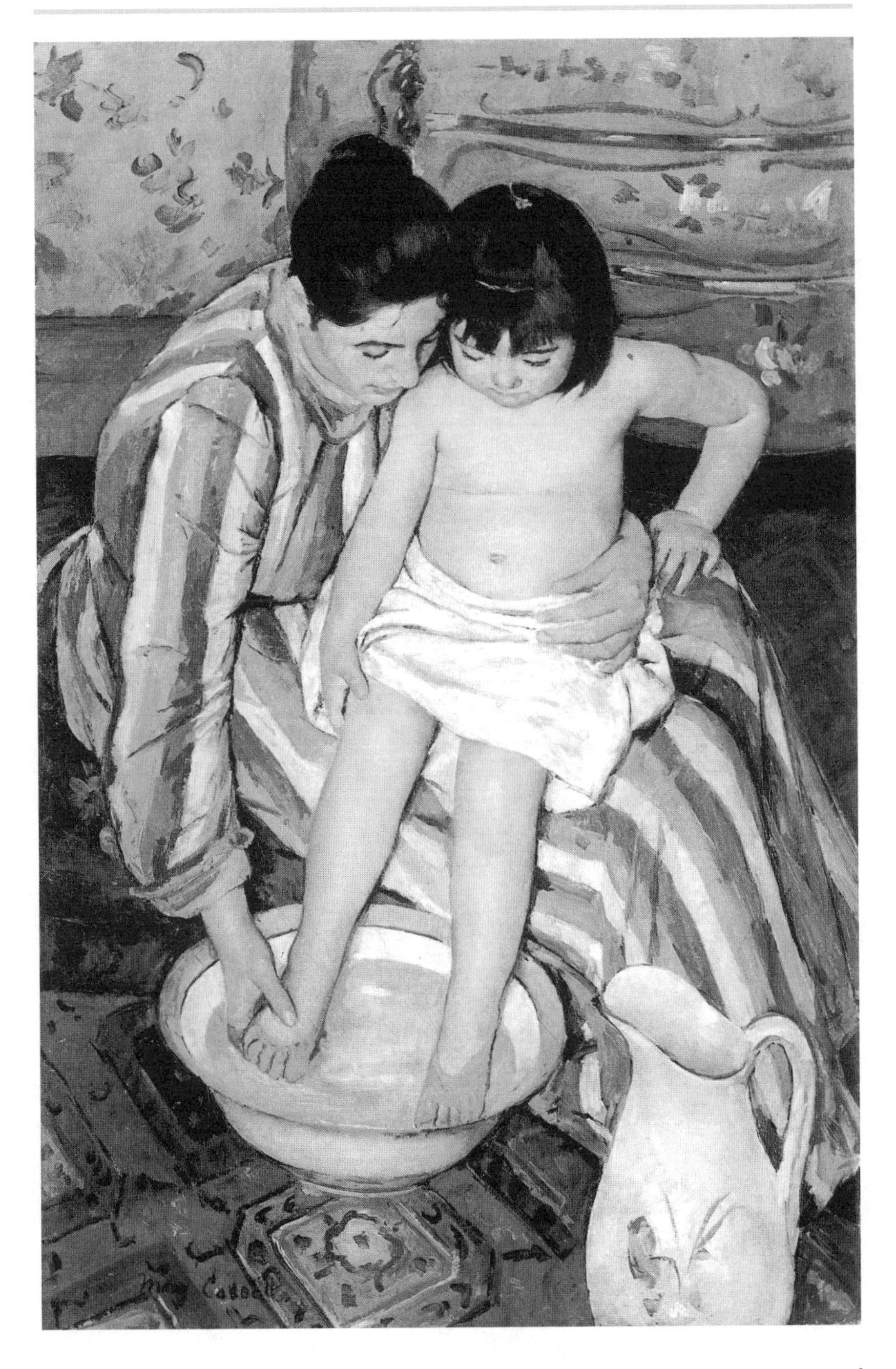

Figure 7 *La Toilette* by Mary Cassatt. Reproduced with permission of Awesome Art.

Further ideas for follow-up work: observational drawing of hands, mixing skin tones

Resources: A4 paper, pencils, paint and palettes

Try to recreate the poses of the hands in the painting. Using your other hand or the hand of a partner, practice drawing hands in a variety of poses. Use pencils, shade the hands and then using a thin paint wash, colour the hands. Practice mixing a realistic 'flesh' colour (adding a small amount of yellow to a pink mix gives a more realistic tone).

Optimistic

Curriculum Links: PSHE 1b **SEAL: Good to be Me**

Literacy: 1a 1b 1c 2b 3c

Learning objectives

- to recognise and appreciate the value of optimism;
- to develop confidence in speaking to an audience and improve performance skills.

Tomorrow arrives like an unexpected letter
From a long forgotten friend.
And the possibilities ahead unfold
Like delicate tissue revealing a special gift.
The day opens like a book
Full of surprises,
Extraordinary characters,
Exciting places,
And happy endings

Vivien Smith

- What does the poet liken a new day to?
- Are there any other similes which could describe a new day?
- Why is the title *Optimistic*?
- What is the opposite of this word?

Further follow-up activities: speaking and listening

With talk partners, describe to each other your perfect day. Share with the rest of the class: Are there any common features? What are they? It is said that everyone is predominantly an optimist or a pessimist. Which do you think you are? Is it better to be an optimist? Why?

Play a circle game. Using appropriate voices pupils alternate round the circle:

'I am an optimist because . . .' (e.g. I'm always smiling).

'I am a pessimist because . . .' (e.g. Every year I think sports day will have to be postponed because it will rain).

Art: 2c 4a 4b 4c

Learning objectives

- to recognise how artists can create texture in their work;
- to be able to create texture in their own work through the technique of weaving.

Vincent van Gogh was a Dutch painter who was born in 1853 and died in 1890. Some of his paintings are amongst the best known in the world and the most expensive. He was a Dutch post-Impressionist. He did not embark on a career as an artist until 1880 but produced more than 2,000 works, 900 paintings and 1,100 drawings and sketches. This painting was produced in 1891. Most of his best-known works were produced in the last two years of his life. During this time he cut off part of his ear after a breakdown in his friendship with Gauguin.

Web image: www.ibiblio.org/wm/paint. Use the artist index to click onto the Van Gogh page. Click onto 'Fields and Cypresses'. The fourth image is *Wheatfield with Rising Sun*.

- How has the artist created texture in this picture?
- What kind of painting technique has he used to produce this effect?
- How many colours can you identify in the sky?
- Do you think this is an optimistic picture? Why/why not?
- In what way does the picture illustrate the poem?

Figure 8 *Wheatfield with Rising Sun* by Vincent van Gogh. Reproduced with permission of Awesome Art.

Further follow-up activities: weaving

Resources: A5 card, wool or string, sellotape, selection of materials (e.g. raffia, leaves and twigs, feathers, ribbon)

Create a weaving board. Using card (about A5 in size), draw vertical lines approximately 1 cm apart. Cut indentations creating a zig-zag effect at top and bottom. Wind wool or string around and secure at the back. Using a selection of materials, both natural and man-made (e.g. raffia, leaves, thin twigs, feathers, ribbon, paper strips), create a weaving that represents a landscape of the pupil's choice.

Proud

Curriculum Links: PSHE 1b 4a

SEAL: Going for Goals

Literacy: 1a 1b 1c 2b 3c

Learning objectives

- to build and improve pupil self-esteem;
- to develop visualisation skills;
- to learn or revise instructional texts.

She lifts my model
As if it is made of fragile glass.
She turns it to the window
And admires how the light falls
So perfectly on its walls.

She walks slowly around the room
Placing it in turn
Exactly in the centre of each table,
Reminding everyone
To look and admire until it's gone.

I notice the envy in their eyes
And the disappointment
Revealed in their slumped bodies.
Regret that they didn't take more care;
That it isn't their model just there.

But it's not theirs – it's mine!
And I sit up straighter and taller
And I smile (but not too much)
And I get a feeling I've not had before.
What is it? I'm not quite sure.

Perhaps it's pride.

Vivien Smith

- Close your eyes and try to imagine what the model in the poem is like. How large is it? What colour is it? Is it an actual representation of an object or something abstract?
- Feed back some of the children's suggestions.
- Which words or phrases tell you that the poet is feeling proud?
- Does the poet often feel proud? How do you know?
- Who is holding the model at the start of the poem?
- Why is she handling the model so carefully?
- How do the other pupils in the poem feel? Why?
- Ask the pupil's to draw what they think the model is and write a set of instructions explaining how it could be made.

Further ideas for follow-up activities: speaking and listening

Close your eyes and think of the time when you have felt really proud of yourself. Was it for something you've made, or done or achieved? When and where was the occasion? Can you describe how you felt? Talk to your partner about it. Share with the rest of the class.

Have you ever made anyone else feel proud by complimenting them in any way?

(Tell the class you are going to give stickers which say 'Ask me what I've done today to make me feel proud'. You are going to give these out for appropriate things achieved. When they are wearing them they must tell anyone who asks what they have done. Prompt other adults in school that this will be happening and they must ask if they see anyone with one of these stickers, thus further building self-esteem. This also creates a further link between home and school.)

Figure 9 *Hill House Chair* by Charles Rennie Mackintosh. Reproduced by kind permission of Antonia Reeve, National Trust for Scotland.

Curriculum Links: PSHE 1b 4a **SEAL: Going for Goals**

Art: 2c 4a 4b 4c

Learning objectives

- to learn about the work of Charles Rennie Mackintosh
- to develop design skills;
- to work from your design to make a model.

Charles Rennie Mackintosh was born in Glasgow in 1868. He was apprenticed to an architect aged sixteen. In 1941 he moved to London where he painted and created textiles. While working in architecture he developed his own style, which often included extensive specification for detail, decoration and the furnishing of the building. He designed *Hill House* in Helensburgh for Walter Blackie, a wealthy publisher. He married Margaret MacDonald who was a fellow artist and collaborator.

Web image: Type *Hill House Chair* by Charles Rennie Mackintosh into your search engine. A choice of images of the chair is available.

Using talk partners, describe this chair to each other and explain why or why not you like it. Feed back to the class.

- Who or what do you think it would be designed for?
- Why do you think the designer chose to construct the chair in this way?
- How comfortable do you think it is to sit on?
- Read the poem again. What line in the poem makes a link with this picture?

Further ideas for follow-up activity: furniture design

Resources: A4 paper, pencils, assortment of materials to produce a prototype if appropriate

On paper, design your own chair in detail. Think about:

- Who would use it and why?
- What materials would be used?
- What colours would be used?

If it is appropriate the children could then construct a prototype using available materials.

Resilient

Curriculum Links: PSHE 1a 1b 1c **SEAL: Going for Goals**

Literacy: 1a 1b 1c 2b 3c

Learning objectives

- developing an understanding of 'resilience' and how it can be developed;
- to understand and use personification.

I'm a window that can never be smashed.
I'm a car that can never be crashed.
I'm a tree that can never be chopped.
I'm a balloon that can never be popped.
I'm a cup that can never be cracked.
I'm a computer that can never be hacked.
I'm a shirt that can never be ripped.
I'm a pancake that can never be flipped.
I'm armour without a dent.
I'm money that's never spent.

Vivien Smith

- Which is your favourite line of the poem and why?
- What does the word 'resilient' mean? (being able to recover easily from misfortune or hurt)
- What is the opposite of resilient?
- Do you think you're resilient or easily hurt?

- What kind of things 'get' to people? Why?
- Are there any strategies we can use to help stop this happening?

Further ideas for follow-up activities: using personification in a poem

- Discuss what personification means and why some writers use it. What effect does it have?
- Ask the class to think of an object they can liken themselves to and explain why they chose this object. It would be good if the teacher could think of one which would describe him/herself, e.g. I think I am like a roundabout because I think about things over and over again and never seem to come to a decision. Things keep going round and round in my mind.
- Discuss with talk partners and share as a class.
- Ask the children to think of at least four objects they can liken themselves to and why and try to write them down in poem form.

Art: 2c 4a 4b 4c

Learning objectives

- to learn about cubism;
- to understand primary colours.

The Builders by Fernand Leger

This is an image of a series of coloured metal girders and ladders representing scaffolding. Six men are working on the scaffolding which is set against a very bright blue sky.

Fernand Leger was a French painter, sculptor and film-maker. He was born in 1881 and died in 1955. Before moving to Paris in 1900 he trained as an architect. This painting was produced in 1950 and is in the Cubist style. He was one of several artists who formed the Puteaux Group, an offshoot of the Cubist movement. He was profoundly affected by his experiences in the First World War, after which he entered a 'mechanical period', when the figures and objects he painted had tubular, machine-like forms.

Web image: Log onto www.orange.co.uk (or use your own preferred search engine, e.g. Google). Click on the image tab above the search box then type in '*The Builders* by Fernand Leger'. Click on one of the images to enlarge.

- What kind of place do you think the artist had in mind when he produced this picture?
- What type of lines has the artist used in the picture? (horizontal and vertical)
- What effect does this have? (maybe they will suggest strong, hard, sturdy)
- Can you describe the figures you can see in the picture and the tasks they are undertaking?
- What colours has the artist used? Do you know what these colours are called? (primary colours – teachers give explanation if necessary, explanation in the Glossary)

Further ideas for follow-up work: wax resistant pictures

Resources: A4 paper, a selection of wax crayons, a selection of sharp instruments (knife, scissors, etc.)

Wax resistant pictures based on one of the objects pupil chose for their poem. Use A4 white paper. Ask pupils to cover the whole sheet with primary coloured wax crayons. Press on quite hard. Next, pressing on hard again, cover colours with black wax crayon. Take a sharp instrument, e.g. blade of knife, or scissors or compass point, and scratch out the chosen image revealing multi-colours underneath.

12

Successful

Curriculum Links: PSHE 1a 1b **SEAL: Going for Goals**

Literacy: 1a 1b 1c 2b 3c

Learning objectives

- to build and improve pupil self-esteem;
- to develop research skills;
- to develop ability to write biographical text.

What does it mean to be successful?
Can it ever be defined?
Is it something to do with money?
Is it very hard to find?

Do I know anyone I think is successful?
What makes them so in my eyes?
Is it something to do with being famous?
How hard did they have to try?

Can I make myself successful?
Is there a magical formula to use?
Is it being fantastic at one thing or another?
Or being determined to win, not lose?

I wonder, does anyone think *I'm* successful?
I wonder why they might think I am?
Do I think of *myself* as successful?
I don't know – I'd better ask me mam.

Vivien Smith

- Ask the pupils for their definition of 'successful'. Talk with a partner.
- Class should feed back suggestions – record on board.
- Ask someone to look for the definition in a dictionary.
- Ask for suggestions of people who the pupils think are successful (it doesn't have to be somebody famous, someone they know perhaps) and why they think they are successful. Do they agree with the suggestions in the poem?
- Why? Why not?
- Is it important to be successful? Why? Why not?
- Ask the pupils to work with their partners. Tell your partner one way in which you think you are successful.
- Try to encourage a very broad spectrum of thought, e.g. being successful at making friends, organisation, responsibility.

Further ideas for follow-up activities: biographical writing

- Revise the use of question marks.
- What effect does the last line have?
- Why do the pupils think the poet has ended the poem this way?
- Ask the pupils to research a person whom they think is successful and write a short biography of them (this could be done in pairs). Include why they think they have become successful.

Art: 2c 4a 4b 4c

Learning objectives

- to learn about the work of Degas;
- to improve and develop design and painting skills.

Figure 10 *Jockey Forward Flexed Standing in the Saddle* by Edgar Degas. Reproduced with permission of Awesome Art.

Edgar Degas was a French painter who was born in 1834 and died in 1917. He was the son of a wealthy banker with an aristocratic background. He was a master of drawing moving human figures and worked in many mediums although he preferred pastels. He exhibited with the Impressionists and was best known for his pictures of horses and ballerinas. Ballet dancers became his favourite theme from the early 1870s. He used to sketch from live models in his studios and then combine his sketches into paintings of various groupings (rehearsing, performing, bending, resting, etc.).

Web image: www.awesome-art.biz. Click onto 'Edgar Degas' in left-hand-column. Scroll down the page to the titles of the paintings and click onto *Jockey Forward Flexed Standing in the Saddle.*

- What medium do you think the artist has used to produce this picture?
- Why do you think the artist hasn't drawn the whole horse?
- Do you think he has been successful in creating the image of a powerful creature? If so how has he managed to achieve this?
- Do you think the jockey is male or female?
- At which point in the race do you think this is? Why do you think this?
- How do you think the jockey is feeling at this point?
- Do you like this picture? Why or why not?

Further follow-up activities: clothing design

Resources: A4 paper, pencils and paints

- Do you know how you can recognise the different horses and jockeys in a race?
- Do you know the special name for the clothes the jockey wears? (silks)
- Look at some examples of jockey silks from the web/books.
- Ask the children to design and paint their own silks.
- Try to encourage the pupils to produce a design which in some way is a reflection of themselves.

Negative emotions

Learning objectives

The following learning objectives relate to the renewed Primary Literacy Framework. Objectives from the framework that are specific to each session appear in the text box at the top of each unit, but all the sessions in this book will enable practitioners to address the following learning outcomes:

Speaking

To be able to:

1a) Offer reasons and evidence for their views considering alternative opinions.
1b) Respond to the contributions of others in the light of differing viewpoints.
1c) Use the technique of dialogic talk to explore ideas topics or issues.

Listening and responding

To be able to:

2b) Follow up others' points and show they agree or disagree in whole class discussion.

Group discussion and interaction

To be able to:

3c) Use the language of possibility to investigate and reflect on feelings, behaviour or relationships.

All the sessions will also enable practitioners to address the following learning outcomes from the Programme of Study for Art and Design. Objectives from the framework that are specific to individual sessions appear in the text box at the top of each unit.

Investigating and making

To be able to:

2c) Use a variety of methods and approaches to communicate observational ideas and feelings and design and make images and artefacts.

Knowledge and understanding

To know about:

4a) Visual and tactile elements including colour, pattern and texture, line and tone shape, form and space.

4b) Materials and processes used in making art and design.

4c) Differences and similarities in the work of artists, craftspeople and designers in different times and cultures (for example sculptors, photographers, architects and textile designers).

Angry

Curriculum Links: PSHE 1a 1d **SEAL: Getting On and Falling Out**

Learning objectives

- to recognise that anger is a destructive emotion and to be able to develop strategies to deal with angry feelings;
- to understand the power of imagery;
- to develop dramatic technique to explore emotions.

All was blue skies
When suddenly the black cloud appeared
And dropped its acid rain,
Penetrating my brain
And exploding inside.
My eyes turned to blood
And my mouth spat out grotesque words
That no-one understood.

Jagged fragments hurtled south
'Til my chest heaved
And my hands scattered like leaves
On a hurricane day.
My legs jerked as if possessed
By an ugly force
Taking its course through my body.

And then it was gone
As quickly as it came
And I became
Weak, puzzled
And
Alone

Vivien Smith

- Why do you think the black cloud suddenly appeared?
- What might have made the poet so angry?
- Why do you think the last word of the poem is 'alone'?
- Can you explain how you feel when you're angry?
- Do you think other people know when you're angry? How?
- Can you suggest any strategies we can use to diffuse angry feelings?

Further ideas for follow-up work: drama

- Work with talk partners. Pupil A should 'freeze frame' an angry face. Pupil B should describe how it looks (either orally or in written form). How does this face make you feel/respond? Change over.
- Each pupil can then say the name of their partner in a normal voice and then in an angry voice. The class can consider tone of voice and the non-verbal gestures and body language and how these affect other people.

Art: 2c 4b 4c

Learning objectives

- To learn about and explore the work of John Martin;
- To be able to use poetry as a stimulus for creating their own visual representation of anger.

Figure 11 *The Great Day of Wrath* by John Martin. Reproduced with permission of the Bridgeman Art Library, Private Collection/ © Christopher Wood Gallery, London, UK/ The Bridgeman Art Library.

John Martin was an English painter born in the North East to a poor family. He lived from 1789 to 1854. He was inspired by the work of John Milton, and his huge canvases show biblical subjects on a vast scale and all are intensely dramatic. He painted catastrophic scenes of cities and landscapes. His work influenced J. M. W. Turner amongst others.

Web image: Log onto www.orange.co.uk (or use your preferred search engine, e.g. Google). Click the images tab above the search box then type in *The Great Day of Wrath* by John Martin. Click on an image to enlarge.

- Give pupils the title of the painting. Do you know what 'wrath' means?
- John Martin painted it to illustrate the Day of Judgement. Does anyone know what is meant by that?
- Can you think of an alternative title?
- What has the artist used in his painting which conveys anger?
- If you were there what might you hear? Smell? Taste?
- How does the picture make you feel? Do you like the painting? Why/why not?

Further follow-up ideas: collage

Resources: A3 paper, collage materials and glue

Look at the *Angry* poem. Using the imagery in the poem and working in small groups, create your own collage depicting anger. This could be either abstract or concrete. Use tissue, coloured paper, coloured magazine pages (it does not matter if there are images on the coloured page), material, etc. Give your collage a title.

Confused

Curriculum Links: PSHE 1a 1b 1c 4a **SEAL: Changes**

Literacy: 1a 1b 1c 2b 3c

Learning objectives

- to explore the feeling of confusion through their own experiences or those of others;
- to explore strategies to cope with feelings of confusion;
- to revise the use of adjectives as describing words.

Dreading the next argument,
Impossible situations when
Violent rages explode before my eyes,
Observing parents I've never seen before,
Realising things will never be the same,
Creating a new world for myself –
End of an era.

Vivien Smith

- What does the poet mean by 'Observing parents I've never seen before'?
- What does 'end of an era' mean?
- How do you think the poet is feeling in this situation?
- How could someone in this situation create a 'new world' for themselves?

Further ideas for follow-up work: speaking and listening

With a talk partner discuss any times when you have felt confused about a situation. Write down any adjectives you feel are appropriate to describe the emotion of confusion. (A thesaurus could be used.)

Conscience Alley

All children line up opposite their partners to form a corridor and think of one of the adjectives they listed. Ask for a volunteer to walk down the 'corridor'. As the volunteer moves along everyone else shouts out their chosen word repeatedly. At the end ask the volunteer how they felt during the exercise. Repeat as teacher/class feels necessary.

Ask the class what they think is the opposite of 'confused'.

Have a time of silent reflection when each child visualises a time or place when they feel calm and at peace. Play some appropriate music.

Art: 2c 4a 4b 4c

Learning objectives

- to learn what is meant by an art installation;
- to understand what is meant by the term 'Op Art'.

Outdoor art work at the church in Palos, Pecs in Hungary by Victor Vasarely

This geometric abstract installation of outdoor artwork is composed of a series of cubes placed at odd angles. The whole piece is made up of orange and blue squares.

Victor Vasarely was born in 1906 and died in 1997. He was a Hungarian French painter and is often described as the father of Op Art. He developed a style of geometric abstract art working with various materials but with a minimal number of forms and colours.

Explain that this is a 3D outdoor installation.

Web image: Use Wikipedia (www.wikipedia.org). Click on the English arrow at the bottom of the page. Click on the multimedia tab in the centre of the page and type "Vasarely" in the search box above. The image is the 6th one on the left hand side of the page. CLick on the image to enlarge it.

- What can you see in the picture?
- If you could fold the top shape over the bottom one, what would you see?
- Does it remind you of anything?
- It is called Op Art. (Information regarding Op Art is in the Glossary.) What do you think the 'op' stands for? What does it mean? (Teacher can show pupils examples of Op Art by other artists, e.g. Bridget Riley.)
- What colours has Vasarely used?

Further ideas for follow-up work: 3D installation

Resources: building kits, assorted boxes, and/or squared paper for net work

- Create your own Op Art installation. Class could be divided into groups each working with different media, e.g. building blocks, construction kits, collection of different sized cardboard boxes.
- Use squared paper. Using a net template cut out several shapes, colour and fold and experiment.

3 Dejected

Curriculum Links: PSHE 1a 1b 1d **SEAL: Good to be Me**

Literacy: 1A 1B 1C 2B 3C

Learning objectives

- to develop self-esteem by being able to cope with negative feelings;
- to develop skill in story planning and narrative writing.

How come I'm never the winner?
Pipped at the post on Sport's Day,
Number never drawn in the raffle,
Don't ever get to hold the trophy?
I'm really baffled.

How come I'm never chosen,
To read out my work,
To play the leading part,
To be on the team?
I mustn't take it to heart.

How come I'm never the favourite,
Of my teacher,
Of my friends,
Of my parents?
It drives me round the bend.

Suppose I should . . .
Try harder,
Smile wider,
Laugh louder,
Just be myself?

Vivien Smith

- What kind of things make the poet feel a failure?
- How does it make them feel?
- What kind of things does the poet think might help change the situation?
- Why do you think the last line has a question mark after it?

Further ideas for follow-up work: play scripts

- In pairs discuss times when you have lost, not been chosen, etc.
- Have a show of hands as to who has ever won:
  - a competition
  - a race
  - a prize

  (hopefully showing that the majority of people never win)
- In pairs devise a story/play about someone who almost wins something. Write or just tell the story.

Art: 2c 4a 4b 4c

Learning objectives

- to learn about the work of Modigliani;
- to develop skill in portrait drawing and working in the style of Modigliani.

Figure 12 *The Boy* by Amedeo Modigliani. Reproduced with permission of the Bridgeman Art Library, Indianapolis Museum of Art, USA/ Gift of Mrs Julian Bobbs in memory of William Ray Adams/ The Bridgeman Art Library/out of copyright.

Amedeo Modigliani was an Italian painter and sculptor who was born in 1884 and died in 1920. He settled in Paris in 1906 and from 1915 concentrated on painting. His interest in African masks and sculpture is evident in his work – his portraits are flat and mask-like with almond eyes, twisted noses and elongated necks. The Boy was painted in 1918.

Web image: Log onto www.ibiblio.org.wm/paint. Use the artist index to find Modigliani. Scroll down the images to find *The Boy* and click on image to enlarge.

- What is it about this portrait which makes the boy look so dejected?
- What do you notice about the colours Modigliani has used?
- What do you notice about the way the facial features and the neck have been painted?
- Can you think of an alternative title for the painting?

Further ideas for follow-up work: portraits

Resources: A4 paper and a range of drawing materials

Work in pairs. Ask your partner to strike a pose of dejection. Experimenting with a range of pencils, sketch your partner. Now using pastels and/or charcoal and chalk, take this sketch and recreate it in the style of Modigliani (see notes above).

4 Disappointed

Curriculum Links: PSHE 1a 1b **SEAL: Good to be Me**

Literacy: 1a 1b 1c 2b 3c

Learning objectives

- to understand that everyone experiences disappointment;
- to widen pupil vocabulary;
- to develop skill in performance poetry.

We were united
All excited
Then it was decided
And now we're divided.

Down to four,
I stare at the floor
Don't want to be ignored.
Down to four.

Please let it be me.
Now there's only three.
I'm the best,
Anyone would agree.
Please let it be me.

Now there's just two . . .
Please don't let it be you.

I've just got to get through.
Please don't let it be you.

I got right to the end,
But it's happened again.
They've chosen my friend.
I got right to the end.

Not selected.
Been rejected.
Feel dejected.
Life's an elective.

Vivien Smith[1]

- What is being decided on in the poem?
- How has the poet's mood changed from the first verse to the last verse? Why?
- Discuss with a partner the meaning of the four verbs used in the last verse. Feed back.
- Give the actual meanings of the words if the children don't know. What do you think the last line really means?
- What is the rhyming pattern of the poem? What effect does this rhyming pattern have? (helps build the speed to a final climax)
- Have you ever been in this position of not being chosen for something? How did it make you feel?
- Can you think of any other times when you've been disappointed? Share with a partner. Share with the class.

Further ideas for follow-up work: performance poetry

Divide the class into groups of five. Each group should practice chanting the poem, trying to achieve this feeling of building to a climax. Have a selection of percussion instruments which can be used to help emphasise the rhythm and use the voices to communicate the change of mood.

[1] Reproduced with permission of Routledge, from *Using Circle Time for PSHE and Citizenship*, Daphne Gutteridge and Vivien Smith (Routledge 2008)

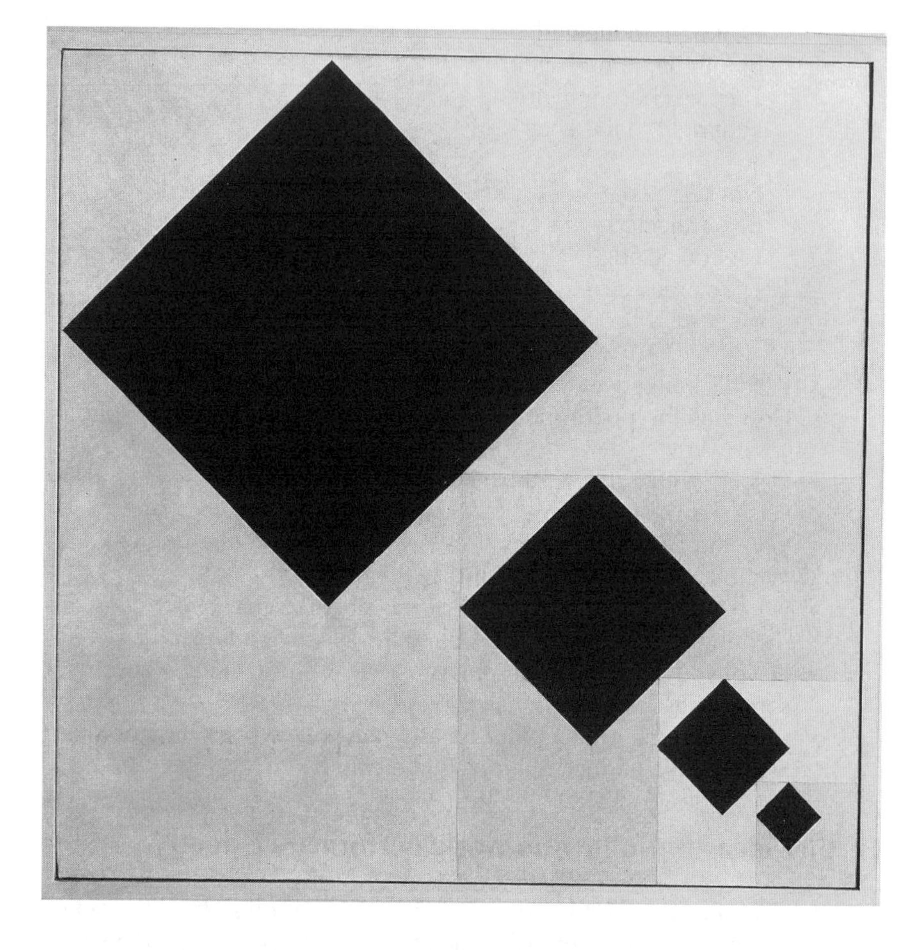

Figure 13 *Arithmetic Composition* by Theo van Doesburg, 1929–1930. Reproduced with permission of the Bridgeman Art Library, Felix Witzinger, Switzerland/ The Bridgeman Art Library/out of copyright.

Art: 2c 4a 4b 4c

Learning objectives

- to develop understanding of perspective in artwork;
- to develop ICT skills through artwork;
- to be able to use a ruler to measure accurately;
- to be able to identify and draw 2D shapes in different orientations.

Theo van Doesburg was a Dutch artist. He was born in 1883 and died in 1931 from a heart attack. He trained as an actor and singer but then decided to become a painter. His first exhibition was in 1908 and his early work was strongly influenced by Van Gogh, both in style and subject matter. He then read a book by Kandinsky about his life as a painter and embraced an abstract style in which many of his pictures featured diagonals. He was a close friend of Mondrian.

Web image: Log onto www.orange.co.uk (or use your own preferred search engine, e.g. Google). Click on the image tab above the search box. Type in *Arithmetic Composition* by Van Doesburg to access the image. Click on an image to enlarge.

- How has the artist created a feeling of movement?
- Do you know what perspective means?
- How has the artist created perspective in this artwork?
- Give out photocopies of the work and let the children measure the sides of each square and the distance between each square. What do they notice?
- Can you discover a link between the picture and disappointment? (The squares are diminishing in size, just as the poet's self-esteem was diminishing as they were being rejected for the team.)

Further ideas for follow-up work: computer/graphic design

Resources: computer and/or A3 paper, rulers, coloured paper

ICT : Working in pairs or small groups, choose a shape and create a similar composition where the shapes are diminishing in size.

Alternatively, the children could create a similar design as above by using simple mathematical calculations, cutting the shapes from coloured paper.

5

Embarrassed

Curriculum links: PSHE 1a 1b **SEAL: Going for Goals**

Literacy: 1a 1b 1c 2b 3c

Learning objectives

- to be able to deal with and move on from difficult situations;
- to develop skill in poetry analysis.

My face is hot and red
I toss and turn in my bed
I go over it in my head,
The stupid things I said.
Why did I do that?

They'll all be laughin' at me.
It's about as bad as it could be.
No way of breakin' free
Of that awful memory.
Why did I do that?

It started out as an ordinary day
I can't believe I acted that way
Now I'm gonna have to pay
But got no choice – I've gotta stay.
Why did I do that?

Vivien Smith

- What do you think the poet did or said to make them feel so embarrassed?
- What do you think the poet meant by 'I'm gonna have to pay'?
- Why do you think people do or say embarrassing things?
- Is there anything the poet could do or say afterwards to make the situation any better?

Further ideas for follow-up work: autobiographical writing

Ask the pupils to think of any embarrassing moments they've ever had. Give each pupil a piece of paper and ask them to write a short account of what happened.

When everyone has finished, hand round an envelope in which the accounts can be put. Explain that you are going to take the envelope away and destroy it along with their accounts. Also explain that this can be a way of them 'letting go' of some things that they would perhaps rather forget.

At the end, ask if anyone wants to share their embarrassing moment, because they can now see the funny side of it themselves. Perhaps the teacher has something they could share with the class also, reinforcing the fact that these things can happen to adults as well.

Art: 2c 4a 4b 4c

Learning objectives

- to learn about the work of Giuseppe Arcimboldo;
- to develop skill in observational still-life drawing.

Vertumnus. A portrait of Rudolf 11 (Holy Roman Emperor) by Giuseppe Arcimboldo

The painting shows an image consisting of the head and shoulders of the Emperor made up of fruit, vegetables and flowers.

Giuseppe Arcimboldo was born in Milan in 1527 and died in 1593. This painting was executed in 1590. His portraits of human heads made up of tree roots, vegetables and fruit were greatly admired by his contemporaries. They continue to fascinate people today. Some people thought that this work was the result of insanity but other scholars think they are examples of the times in which he lived when people were fascinated by puzzles, riddles and the bizarre.

Web image: Use Wikipedia (www.wikipedia.org). Type 'Giuseppe Arcimboldo' in the search box. The image appears on his page. Click on it to enlarge the image.

- In pairs list the flowers, fruits and vegetables you can see in the picture. Feed back and record.
- What is used to produce the facial features, the hair, the body?
- Why do you think the artist produced paintings like these?
- What do you think people at the time might have thought about them?
- What do you think about this painting?

Further ideas for follow-up work: observational drawing and collage

Resources: A4 paper, a selection of fruit, vegetables, flowers, coloured pencils, scissors and glue

- Have three tables set up for observational drawing: a selection of fruit, flowers and vegetables.
- Divide the class into three groups and rotate the groups so they have an opportunity to draw all three objects.
- Use coloured pencils and/or oil pastels.
- Ask the pupils to cut out their drawings and create an object of their choice from these. It might be a face or it could be anything else they choose, a car, musical instrument, etc. Alternatively pictures of flowers, fruits and vegetables could be cut from magazines and used, or a mixture of the two.

Fearful

Curriculum Links: PSHE 1a 1c **SEAL: Going for Goals**

Literacy: 1a 1b 1c 2b 3c

Learning objectives

- to encourage pupils to express their feelings and share coping strategies;
- to revise similes and metaphors;
- use dramatic techniques to explore an emotion.

Stomach churning
Like a washing machine
Mouth as dry
As smooth shells
Body tingling
Like a sand storm in a dessert
Ears ringing
Like a hundred church bells.
Mind racing
Like fast forward music
Breath as rapid
As a thirsty dog
Eyes unblinking
Like a lifeless corpse
Ready to run
Like an athlete in the blocks

Vivien Smith

- Can you describe how you feel when you are very frightened?
- What kind of things make you feel afraid?
- Can anyone share a strategy they have used to help them overcome their fear? (Take deep breaths, repeat a calming mantra, etc.)
- What do you call the phrases that appear in every other line? (simile)
- Do you know what a metaphor is and how is it different to a simile? (Teacher to explain if necessary)
- Change each simile to a metaphor, e.g. my stomach was a churning washing machine on a busy day.
- Which is your favourite line and why?

Further ideas for follow-up activities: drama

The class stands in a circle. Ask for a volunteer to stand in the centre and make a freeze frame of being very afraid, and to think of a reason why they might feel frightened. Children take turns to ask questions about what is making the person in the centre so afraid and how they might be feeling.

Ask all the children to make the same freeze frame. Can they feel the tension in their bodies? Then, starting from their toes and working upwards, ask the children to try to relax each part of their body. (Music could be used.) How do they feel now?

Art: 2c 4a 4b 4c

Learning objectives

- to explore artwork from a different culture;
- to develop skill in designing and mask making.

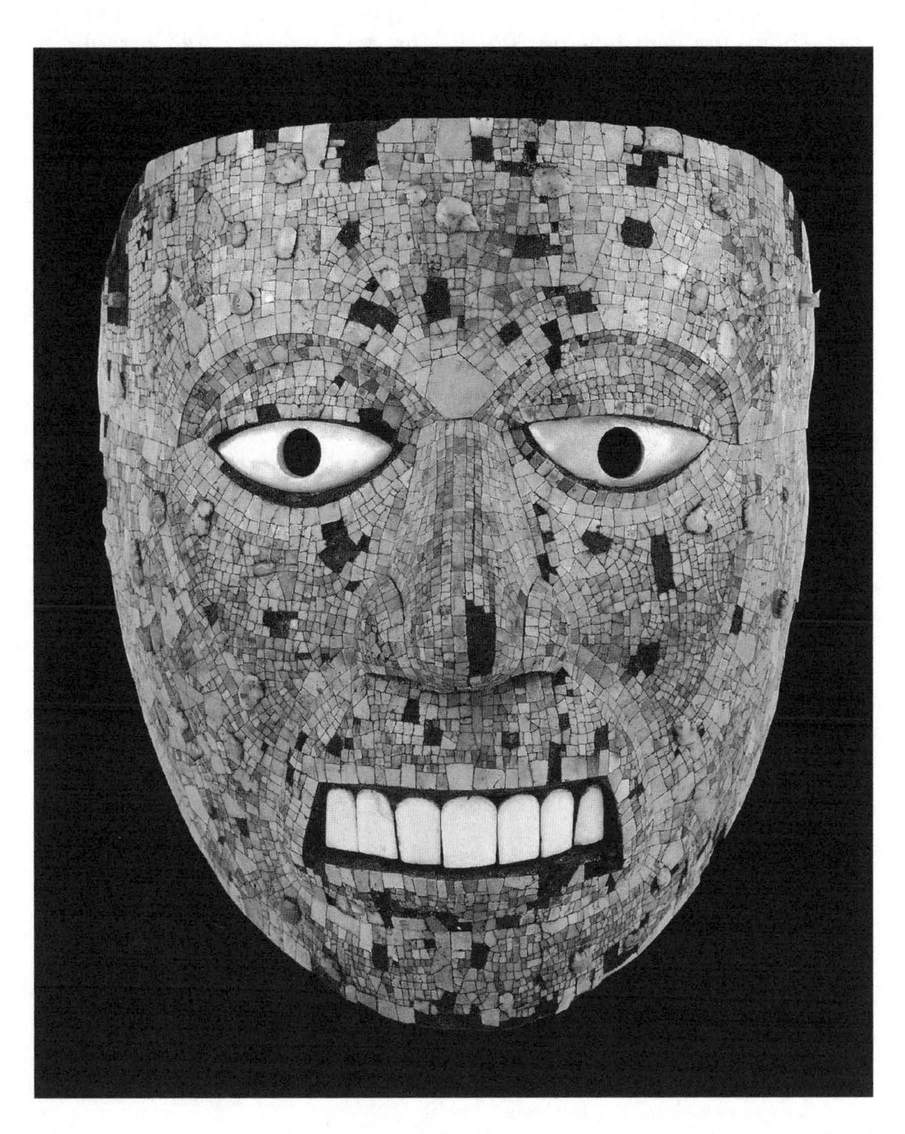

Figure 14 *Aztec Mask of Xiuhtecuhti* (circa 1500). Reproduced by kind permission of The Trustees of the British Museum.

Masks are artefacts that have been used since antiquity by many cultures. They were used for ceremonial and practical purposes often connected with religious rituals. The Aztecs prized human skulls as war trophies and masks made from human skulls have been found.

Web image: www.bmimages.com. Click on 'Africa, Oceania and Americas' tab in 'browse our collections'. Scroll down and click on the mask to enlarge.

- Which parts of the mask are most fearsome? Why?
- Why do you think the artist has chosen these particular colours for the mask?
- For what reason do you think the mask was made?
- Would you be afraid if you saw a person wearing this mask? Why?

Further ideas for follow-up work: mosaic masks

Resources: paper plates and/or card or balloons, paper, glue, a selection of shiny gummed paper and scissors

Design your own mask. Make it really fearsome. The mask can be made from a paper plate or curved card. Alternatively papier mâché placed on a blown-up balloon could used. Use coloured shiny gummed paper roughly cut into small squares to cover the mask to create a mosaic effect.

Frustrated

Curriculum Links: PSHE 1a 1d **SEAL: Getting On and Falling Out**

Literacy: 1a 1b 1c 2b 3c

Learning objectives

- to identify feelings associated with frustration and develop strategies to cope with these feelings;
- to understand the use of imagery in poetry.

Purple, blue, green and red,
Colouring the whole of me.
An abstract painting
Inside my head.

Fireworks exploding
In my brain
Washing my body
With psychedelic rain.

I want to run and run
And never cease.
I'm trapped in a nightmare
With no sign of peace.

I open my mouth
But there is no sound,

Like a silent film

Whirring round and round.

'Til at last it comes

I'm released from my dream

And I scream

And

Scream

And

Scream

And

S

C

R

E

A

M

Vivien Smith

- What may have made the person feel so frustrated? Have you ever felt like this?
- Can anyone suggest strategies we could use to help us calm down when we feel like this?
- Discuss what we mean by the word 'imagery' in relation to poetry? Discuss the imagery the poet has used verse by verse.
- How has the poet chosen to make the last verse different? What effect does it create?

Further ideas for follow-up work: drama

- Discuss with talk partners what situations make you feel frustrated and why you may be unable to do anything about them?
- Having given the class discussion time, take feedback on four or five situations that they have identified. The pupils can reflect on these, then vote on which they would find the most frustrating.
- Divide the class into small groups. They can then enact the four/five situations.

Art: 2c 4b 4c

Learning objectives

- to familiarise the children with the work of Edvard Munch;
- to develop a 3D sculpture inspired by a 2D piece of art.

The Scream by Edvard Munch 1893

This famous image shows the upper body of a stark figure holding his hands over his ears. His mouth is open wide as if screaming. The background is an abstract impression of sea/sky

Edvard Munch was a Norwegian painter and printmaker. He was born in 1863 and died in 1944. He was a major influence in German Expressionism. The Scream (sometimes called The Cry) was painted in 1893 and is regarded as an iconic painting of anguish. His work often included symbolic portrayal of themes like misery, sickness and death. The Scream is probably his most famous canvas and is a typical example of his expression of anguish, fear and isolation.

Web image: Log onto www.orange.co.uk (or use your preferred search engine, e.g. Google). Click on the images tab above the search box. Type in *The Scream* by Munch. Then click on an image to enlarge.

- Allow the children a few minutes to look at the picture in silence. Ask them for their immediate thoughts on it. How does it make them feel?
- Who do they think the character is? Why are they screaming?
- Explain that this is a famous artwork. Ask them why they think it is so famous.
- What can they see in the background? What is the mood of this picture?
- What kind of lines or strokes has the artist used to create this mood?

Further ideas for follow-up work: sculpture

Resources: air dry clay and clay tools, coloured paper, pencil and scissors

Ask the children to close their eyes and imagine they can see and hear someone screaming. What colours can they see? What shapes can they see? Are there straight or curved lines or both?

Using clay, create the face they have imagined. While the clay is drying ask the children to cut out the letters of the word 'scream'. They can do this anyway they want, choose any colour or pattern the letters. When the clay is dry, position the head on a piece of paper and arrange the letters around the sculpture. It doesn't have to be horizontal or the letters necessarily in the right order. Encourage them to be experimental.

Jealous

Curriculum Links: PSHE 1a 1d **SEAL: Getting On and Falling Out**

Learning objectives

- to raise pupil self-esteem;
- to understand that feeling jealous is a natural emotion;
- to understand what an autobiography is and to develop skill in writing in an autobiographical genre.

I was sitting at my desk, minding my own business
When the green blob tapped me on my shoulder
And pointed at Jenny Webster.
Her hair hung down, shiny, blond and straight;
Mine's curly and brown, everything about it I hate!

I was standing shivering on the games field
When 'Green' appeared and turned to the right.
There was Anna Cyrek
Jumping up and down with glee
She'd scored the winning goal – not me!

I was just about to get on the bus
When I heard a shout and a pair of green eyes
Swivelled towards the road.
Jaspal Samad was climbing into a brand new 4 × 4.
We've got a clapped out micra with a dent in the door.

Christmas party – I thought I looked pretty good
'Til the green beast arrived and smirked over at the door.
Amy Dobson strolled in
Wearing skinny jeans and a sparkly top.
My dress was last year's from the catalogue shop.

What can I do to rid myself of the 'man in green'?
He makes me feel disgruntled. He makes me feel so mean.
I'm not that unhappy, really I'm not
So why am I worried by this blob of green snot?
It's not good to feel jealous. Envy's a sin.
Mustn't let him get to me. Can't let him win.

Vivien Smith

- Who or what is the 'man in green'?
- Jealousy appears as a person. What effect does this have?
- What kind of things do the pupils think the poet is jealous of?
- How does feeling jealous make the poet feel?
- Everyone feels jealous at some time or another – how can we help ourselves not to feel jealous so 'he' doesn't win?
- Share with a partner any times you have been jealous and how it made you feel.
- Ask if anyone has heard the sayings 'green with envy' and 'the green-eyed monster'. Ask if anyone has any ideas as to why envy or jealousy is associated with the colour green.

Further follow-up activities: autobiographical writing

In a circle ask each pupil to think of a good point about the person next to them. Ask the pupils to write an autographical text concentrating on all the good things about themselves and their life. Put these in a special book to be read by the class or display them for others to read.

Art: 2c 4a 4b 4c

Learning objectives

- to understand how artists can use nature to help create feelings within a picture;
- to use natural forms as inspiration for their own designs.

Figure 15 *A Beautiful Flower* by Lawrence Alma-Tadema. Reproduced with permission of Awesome Art.

Lawrence Alma-Tadema was born in the Netherlands 1836. He died in 1912 and is buried in St Paul's Cathedral. He trained in Belgium, and at the age of fifteen he suffered a physical and mental breakdown and was diagnosed as a consumptive. He settled in England in 1870 where he spent the rest of his life. He was a classical subject painter whose work was universally admired during his lifetime.

Web image: www.awesome-art.biz. Click onto 'Alma-Tadema' on the left hand side. Click onto 'view all images on CD'. The image appears on the second row. Click on it to enlarge.

- What do you think the dark-haired woman is thinking as she looks at the blonde girl? Where do you think they are and what might they be doing there?
- The title is *A Beautiful Flower*. Do you think this refers to the actual flowers or to one of the women?
- Do you like this painting? Why/why not?

Further follow-up activities: paper sculpture

Resources: assorted paper, tissue and card, wire, pipe cleaners

Have a selection of real flowers, leaves, grasses and/or photographs. After looking at them the children could design and construct their own flower/leaf/grass using the resources provided. These could be used for display either grouped in vases or as a 3D wall panel.

Lonely

Curriculum Links: PSHE 1a 1d **SEAL: Changes**

Literacy: 1a 1b 1c 2b 3c

Learning objectives

- to explore the concept of loneliness;
- to develop understanding of how a mood can be created through poetry;
- to develop their own poetry writing using a set structure.

Loneliness is a clearing in a hidden forest,
A lost coin in a hurried street,
An empty seat on a crowded train,
A motionless figure amongst pounding feet.

Loneliness is a clock ticking in an empty room,
The last hum of a computer at the end of the day,
The final note of a song sung alone,
Laughter coming from far away.

Loneliness is the sound of my own heart beating,
My voice speaking to someone who isn't there,
The tap of my soles echoing in a hallway,
And a sigh in the warm night air

Vivien Smith

- What are the similarities and differences of the three verses?
- Which line makes you feel most lonely?
- Do you know what a metaphor is?
- In pairs or as a circle explain when or where you feel most lonely?
- Are there any sights or sounds which you associate with loneliness?
- Is there anything you can do to help make you feel less lonely?
- What do you think is the opposite of 'lonely'? Discuss with the pupils if they think being alone is always a negative thing?

Further ideas for follow-up work: speaking and listening, poetry writing

In a circle, create a 'day in the life of' the person in the Hockney painting. Each child in turn creates the next part of the story.

Create a class poem with each line beginning: Only the lonely . . . e.g. Only the lonely stand by themselves in the playground. This activity could begin with the class sitting in a circle and each using the phrase 'only the lonely' in turn.

Art: 2c 4a 4b 4c

Learning objectives

- to develop understanding of the work of David Hockney as a modern British artist;
- to develop skill in collage work;
- to use story telling as a stimulus for art.

Portrait of Nick Wilder by David Hockney

The portrait shows a very modern expensive house with a swimming pool. The head and shoulders of a lone man can be seen in the pool.

David Hockney was born in 1937. He is a British painter who attended the Royal College of Art and achieved great success by the time he reached his mid-twenties. He is the best known artist of his generation who has spent much time in the USA. The Californian swimming pool has been one of his favourite themes, and this particular picture was painted in 1966. The portrait shows a very modern expensive house with a swimming pool. The head and shoulders of a lone man can be seen in the pool.

Web image: www.ibiblio.org/wm/paint. Use the artist index to click onto 'David Hockney'. Scroll down the page and click on *Portrait of Nick Wilder* to enlarge.

- What can you see in the picture?
- Where do you think this house might be?
- How do you think the man in the picture is feeling?
- There are only two basic colours. What are they?
- Why do you think the artist has limited the colour scheme?
- How many shades of each colour can you see?
- What shapes has the artist used in this picture?

Further ideas for follow-up work: collage work

Resources: A5 paper, tissue, pages form magazines, material, scissors and glue

Using A5 paper, create a collage in shades of one single colour (use tissue, paper and/or pages from magazines, material, etc.). When complete cut out a pair of black footprints and place on the picture.

Alternatively, this could be a group activity using large-scale collage using life-size footprints (pupils can draw around their own feet).

10 Sad

Curriculum Links: PSHE 1a 1c 1d 4g **SEAL: Changes**

Literacy: 1a 1b 1c 2b 3c

Learning objectives

- to explore difficult times in life and to encourage empathy;
- to understand superlatives and develop skill in using a thesaurus;
- to develop vocabulary;
- to understand how a mood can be created in a poem;
- to develop vocabulary.

Sometimes,
When I close my eyes,
I can see you running towards me.
Sometimes,
When I listen extra hard,
I can hear you greeting me as I fling open the door.
Sometimes,
If I really sniff the air, I can smell your warm coat.
Sometimes,
If I stay very still, I can feel your breath hot on my legs
And your soft fur brushing through my fingers.
Sometimes
In the kitchen, I imagine your bowl filled with food
And your basket with the cosy rug.
Sometimes
When I wake, I think your rough tongue is licking my face
And your cold nose is nuzzling under the covers.

Sometimes,
Just as I sleep, I taste the tears
And remember the pain inside my chest
When I whisper your name

Vivien Smith[1]

- Who/what do you think the poet is speaking about? What emotion do you think they're feeling?
- What do you think you could say or do to make them feel better?
- What senses is the poet describing?
- What do we mean when we use the phrase 'pain inside my chest'? (heartache)
- If you close your eyes, can you picture someone or something which is very special to you? Try and imagine how you might feel if they were no longer there.

Further ideas for follow-up activities: thesaurus work

Divide the class into small groups. Using a thesaurus, look up the word 'sorrow'. Can you list the words given in order of intensity? As a whole class share, discuss and record.

Think about a sadness or sorrow in your own life. (Suitable music could be played.) Which words best describe how it makes you feel?

Art: 2c 4a 4b 4c

Learning objectives

- to explore pre-Raphaelite art and its techniques;
- to develop skill in shading.

[1]Reproduced with permission of Routledge from *Using Circle Time for PSHE and Citizenship*, Daphne Gutteridge and Vivien Smith (Routledge 2008)

Figure 16 *Beata Beatrix* by Dante Gabriel Rossetti. Reproduced with permission of Bridgeman Art Library Delaware Art Museum, Wilmington, USA/ Delaware Art Museum Acquisition Fund/ The Bridgeman Art Library/out of copyright.

Dante Gabriel Rossetti was born in 1828 and died in 1882. He was also a poet and love was the main theme of both his poems and paintings. He grieved for the loss of his wife who died in 1862 and spent the last years of his life as a recluse. He idealised her memory using her as a model for this picture, painted after her death in 1863. It hangs in Tate Britain in London.

Web image: www.ibilio.org.wm.paint. Use the artist index to locate Rosetti. Log onto his page, scroll down and click on *Beata Beatrix* to enlarge.

- What objects can you see in the picture? Why do you think the artist has included these things?
- What words from the group lists made in the literacy activity could be used to best describe how Beatrix looks?
- Who do you think the figure in the background might be? Why might he/she be there?
- Describe how Beatrix is holding her hands.
- Can you see the bird in the picture? Why might the painter have included this?
- What can you see to the right of the main figure? (Sundial – ensure they understand what it is.) Why do you think it may be there?
- Why do you think the painter has painted a bright yellow light at the back?

Further ideas for follow-up work: shading/blending /skills

Resources: triangular pieces of paper, pastels/charcoal/chalks

Use a triangular piece of paper create a picture, shading from dark to light, using pastels/charcoal/chalk, blending the colours with fingers or tissue. You can incorporate all or any of the words from the list that were generated in the literacy activity.

Stressed

Curriculum Links: PSHE 1a 1c 1d 4g

SEAL: Getting on and Falling out

Literacy: 1a 1b 1c 2b 3c

Learning objectives

- to recognise the nature of stress and develop strategies to cope with it;
- to develop a wider vocabulary;
- to develop performance skills.

Irritation
Aggravation
Manipulation
Deprivation

Persecution
Execution
Destitution
Retribution

Antagonise
Brutalise
Terrorise
Monopolise

Aggression
Possession
Oppression
Depression

Scattered
Battered
Tattered
Shattered

Vivien Smith

- Divide the class into five groups. Each group take one verse and define the words in the verse.
- Which words apply best when you are feeling stressed?
- How is the last verse different from the others? Why?
- With talk partners, discuss what sort of things make you feel stressed. Can you suggest any strategies for dealing with these feelings? (Share at discretion of teacher)

Further ideas for follow-up work: performance poetry

In your original groups, rehearse and perform the poem as a rap. Encourage varied tones of voice and perhaps include some sound effects.

Art: 2c 4a 4b 4c

Learning objectives

- to develop an understanding of abstract art;
- to be able to produce an abstract painting.

Figure 17 *Fighting Forms* by Franz Marc. Reproduced with permission of Awesome Art.

Franz Marc was born in Munich in 1880. He studied there but travelled to France where he saw the work of the Impressionists. This picture was painted in 1914. He volunteered for military service in the First World War and died during the Battle of Verdun in 1916, aged only thirty-six. Although he died so young, he was a pioneer of abstract art and created some of the most exciting and touching paintings of the abstract movement.

Web image: Log onto www.ibiblio.org/wm/paint and use the artist index to find Marc's page. Scroll down to *Fighting Forms* and click to enlarge the image.

- How do you think Franz Marc was feeling when he painted this picture? Do you think he was stressed? Why/why not?
- How do you think he created it?
- What colours has he chosen? Why do you think he chose these colours?
- Do you like it? Why/why not?

Further ideas for follow-up work: abstract painting

Resources: A3 or A4 paper, paint, palettes, straws, brushes, sticks, etc.

Choose three or four colours to create your own canvas using a variety of techniques including splattering, blowing paint through straws, dragging sticks through paint, using hands/fingers, etc. When the painting is dry, use it as a graffiti wall and choose words from the poem and/or any other stress-related words and write them on the painting.

Threatened

Curriculum Links: PSHE 1a 1b 1c 4a SEAL: Getting on and Falling out

Literacy: 1a 1b 1c 2b 3c

Learning objectives

- to explore feelings connected to difficult situations and share strategies to deal with these;
- to learn about and understand personification;
- to widen pupil vocabulary.

Dark clouds gathered,
Passing over my head
Like the grey blankets on my bed.
An ominous, howling wind arrived
Battering my ears and arousing my fears.
Then it slowly rose from the boiling sea.
Its giant jaws grinding and snapping;
Its jewelled spittle, spurting and spraying over me.
It flaunted its jagged white teeth
And its slavering tongue – long and leering,
Peered at me from the eye of the storm.
I had but a moment to decide:
I could turn, run and hide
Or stand firm and fast,
Trusting that all things do not last.

It finally recedes
And crawls, whimpering and weakened,
Back from whence it came.
Whilst I stand
STRONGER,
TALLER,
PROUDER.

Vivien Smith

- What does the poet liken the sea to? What is it called when an object is described as having human characteristics? (personification)
- Why is the title of the poem 'Threatened'?
- Is it really all about a storm? If not, what is it also about? (teacher could introduce the word 'allegory' and explain its meaning: story symbolizing an underlying meaning.)
- What choices does the poet give in the second verse?
- What would you do?
- Can you think of a time when you felt threatened? Share this with a talk partner.
- Why do we sometimes feel threatened? Can anyone suggest strategies to deal with feeling threatened? Is it always a good idea to stay and face the situation? Why/why not?

Further ideas for follow-up activities: vocabulary extension/dictionary work

In pairs try to guess the meaning of the following words: ominous, arouse, spittle, flaunt, slaver, leer, peer, recede, whence. Share ideas as a class. Now look them up in the dictionary.

Art: 2c 4a 4b 4c

Learning objectives

- to explore the work of Hokusai, an artist from a different culture;
- to learn and use the technique of marbling.

Figure 18 *The Wave* by Katsushika Hokusai. Reproduced with permission of the Bridgeman Art library Private Collection/ Lauros / Giraudon/ The Bridgeman Art Library/out of copyright.

Katsushika Hokusai was a Japanese painter and wood engraver who was born in 1760 and died in 1849. He produced a vast number of book illustrations and colour prints that were inspired by the traditions and legends of the Japanese people. He used large broken strokes and colour choices that gave a sombre mood to his work. This painting is one in a series called 36 Views of Mount Fuji, which were painted between 1823 and 1829.

Web image: www.ibiblio.org/wm/paint. Use the artist index to locate Hokusai. *The Wave* is the first image on his page. Click on the image to enlarge.

- Look at the poem 'Threatened'. Match some of the lines from the first verse to what you can see in the painting.
- Where do you think this artist was when he painted this picture? What makes you think this?
- How many shades of blue can you identify in this painting?
- How does it make you feel when you look at this painting. (Sea music could be played whilst the pupils study the painting.)

Further ideas for follow-up activities: marbling

Resources: A4 size container, marbling inks, A4 paper, straws/ pencils

Create a seascape using the technique of marbling. Fill a plastic or metal shallow tin with water (the container should be a little over A4 size – a cat litter tray is ideal). Using marbling inks (gloss paint also works well but obviously marks clothes and smells), select two, three or four colours. One colour at a time, drop some ink onto the water and swirl the colours around on the water with a straw or pencil. (The colours should float on top.) Carefully, place a piece of A4 paper on top and leave it a few seconds to absorb the ink. Peel off the paper and place flat to dry.

List of artists and artworks

Alma-Tadema, Lawrence (1836–1912) – *A Beautiful Flower*	Jealous
Anon. (circa 1500) – *Aztec Mask of Xiuhtecuhti*	Fear
Anon. (Henry VIII) – *Stained Glass Window of Henry VIII*	Confident
Arcimboldo, Giuseppe (1527–1593) – *Rudolf II*	Embarrassed
Balla, Giacomo (1871-1958) – *Flight of the Swallows*	Determined
Cassatt, Mary (1844–1926) – *La Toilette*	Loved
Degas, Edgar (1834–1917) – *Jockey Forward Flexed Standing in the Saddle*	Successful
Hockney, David (1937–) – *Portrait of Nick Wilder*	Lonely
Hokusai, Katsushika (1760–1849) – *The Wave*	Threatened
Leger, Fernand (1881–1955) – *The Builders*	Resilient
Mackintosh, Charles Rennie (1868–1928) – *Hillhouse Chair*	Proud
Marc, Franz (1880–1916) – *Fighting Forms*	Stressed
Martin, John 1789–1854) – *The Great Day of Wrath*	Anger
Matisse, Henri (1869–1954) – *La Danse*	Happy
Modigliani, Amedeo (1884–1920) – *The Boy*	Dejected
Munch, Edvard (1863–1944) – *The Scream*	Frustrated
Puvis de Chavannes, Pierre (1824–1898) – *Carrier Pigeon*	Hopeful
Rossetti, Dante Gabriel (1828–1882) – *Beata Beatrix*	Sad
Roualt, Georges (1871–1958) – *Christ en Croix*	Brave
Seurat, Georges (1859–1891) – *The Circus*	Excited
van Doesburg, Theo (1883–1931) – *Arithmetic Composition*	Disappointed
Van Gogh, Vincent (1853–1890) – *Wheatfield with Rising Sun*	Optimistic
Vasarely, Victor (1908–) – *Outdoor Work at the Church in Palos*	Confused

Glossary of terms

Abstract art – art not representing recognisable objects or the world around us.
Acrostic – a poetic form that is organised by the initial letters of a key word, either at the beginning of lines, or with lines arranged around them.
Alliteration – a phrase where adjacent or closely connected words begin with the same sound or letter.
Allegory – a story symbolising an underlying meaning.
Aztecs – native people dominant in central Mexico at the time of the Spanish conquest.
Collage – artistic composition in which objects are glued to a backing to form a picture.
Conscience Alley – a drama technique in which the class forms two lines facing each other. One person takes the main role and walks between the lines as each member of the groups speaks their advice. It can also be organised so that those on one side give opposing advice to those on the other. When the person reaches the end of the alley, they make their decision.
Consumptive – a person suffering from tuberculosis.
Cubism – an artistic movement in which artists portray objects as 'flattened' so that different sides of each shape can be shown simultaneously from various angles.
Expressionism – based on artists expressing their innermost feelings in their paintings rather than representing the external world. It is highly personal and intense, using violent colours and dramatic brushwork.
Freeze frame – still images or silent tableaux used to illustrate a specific incident or event. Individual children or groups are asked to represent the characters or a significant moment. The freeze frame can be improvised or planned briefly. Positioning and body shape have to be considered in order to represent ideas or emotions.

Frescoes – pictures painted on walls or ceilings before plaster is dry.
Fauvism – French for 'wild beasts', this artistic movement began in 1905, using strong colours without regard to the natural colour of the subject and dynamic brushwork. The paintings often represented heightened emotion and joy.
Installation art – the use of sculptural materials and any other materials to transform a space or area. It is not necessarily confined to gallery spaces and can be used in everyday public or private spaces.
Imagery – use of language to create a vivid image in the mind.
Impressionism – a style of painting, originating in France in the 1860s, which gives a general impression without detail and explores the relationship between light and colour.
Manikin – small, wooden figure with moveable body parts.
Marbling – a method of water surface design, which can produce patterns similar to those of marble. The patterns are produced by floating colour on water and then carefully transferred to a sheet of paper.
Marouflage – paintings executed on a large canvas, which is then fixed to the wall.
Metaphor – when something is written about as if it were really something else.
Op Art – short for 'optical art', it is used to confuse the human eye. Although static, the forms and colours used cause an optical illusion of movement.
Papier mâché – French for 'chewed-up paper', consists of pieces of paper stuck together using a wet paste, e.g. glue or wallpaper paste. The object becomes solid when the paste dries.
Personification – a form of metaphor in which language relating to human action, motivation and emotion is used to refer to non-human objects or abstract concepts.
Perspective – the relation between visible objects as to position and distance.
Pointillism – a technique whereby the colour is painted onto canvas as dots and when viewed at a distance the dots appear to fuse together.
Pre-Raphaelite – a movement formed in 1848 by young English artists who sought to evoke early Italian art. Pre-Raphaelite pictures often depict historical or religious scenes and make moralising comments.
Primary colours – colours which cannot be created from mixing other colours together: red, yellow and blue. With these three colours and white it is possible to mix most other colours.
Rap – a form of oral poetry which has a very strong rhythm and rapid pace.
Simile – the writer creates an image in readers' minds by comparing a subject to something else.
Sonnet – a poem of fourteen lines; may follow any rhyme scheme.

Stained glass – decorative or pictorial designs made of pieces of glass, either dyed or coloured, set in a lead framework.
Superlative – expressing the highest degree or quality.
Synonym – word or phrase which means exactly the same or very similar to another.
Think, pair, share – children are provided with the opportunity to think about an issue without interruption, then share their thoughts with a 'talk partner'. Ideas can then be shared with the whole class.
Visualisation – forming pictures in the mind.

Index